A Can of ...

A CAN OF TUNA

THE COMPLETE GUIDE TO COOKING WITH TUNA

ANDY BLACK

Prism Press

First published in Great Britain 1995 by
PRISM PRESS
The Thatched Cottage
Partway Lane
Hazelbury Bryan
Sturminster Newton
Dorset DT10 2DP

and distributed in the USA by
ATRIUM PUBLISHERS GROUP
3356 COFFEY LANE
SANTA ROSA
CA 95403

ISBN 1 85327 091 1

© Andy Black 1995

Typeset by Prism Press, Bridport, Dorset
Printed by The Guernsey Press Ltd., C.I.

CONTENTS

5

INTRODUCTION

Tuna, and more specifically canned tuna, is the Cinderella of foodstuffs. It has almost everything going for it, yet it has been systematically ignored by the culinary elite. At its best it has a wonderful flavour; it is inexpensive and universally available; it is high in protein, low in cholesterol and low in calories. Only the egg can compete with it on equal terms. Pound for pound, eggs probably win on cost, but they certainly lose on the health side of the equation. Let's call it a draw.

There is a popular misconception about tuna and it goes something like this: 'Tuna is tuna is tuna and it comes in tins.' Nothing could be further from the truth. Tuna is in fact a generic name used to describe a wide variety of fish which inhabit tropical and sub-tropical waters around the world. These range from the *bluefin*, a magnificent game fish which can weigh upwards of 1500 pounds, to the much smaller *albacore* which is famous for its succulent white meat. Between these extremes there are innumerable other varieties, the most common of which are *yellow fin* and *skipjack*.

To be fair to the misconception, fresh tuna is today something of a rarity, and an expensive rarity at that. The vast majority of the tuna caught around the world is bought by the giant canneries of America, Europe and the Far East. Canned tuna, however, is not a single entity. It comes in a wide variety of types and textures. The easiest way to know exactly what you are getting is to read the label. Firstly this will tell you what colour the fish is. This can range from *white*, to *lightt* to *dark*. As a rule of thumb it is fair to say that the lighter the meat, the better the taste.

Then there is the packing medium. There are three types: olive oil, vegetable oil and brine. Tuna in olive oil unquestionably has the best flavour and texture, but brine packed tuna has the advantage of being lower in calories and cholesterol. From the point of view of cooking, they are virtually interchangeable and in the following pages, the packing medium is only specified when it has a direct effect on the dish concerned.

The third consideration when buying a tin of tuna is the texture of the meat packed. This comes in four types: *solid pack* which is generally a single piece of meat; *chunk* which is made up of large pieces of meat - this is ideal for salads and dishes where a certain body is desirable. Next down the line comes *flake* which comprises smaller less desirable pieces of meat. This is fine for casseroles and baked dishes where the flavour is more important than texture. Finally there is *grated*. This tends to be something of a mush and is best avoided except for pates, mousses and sauces.

Over the years, tuna has received a bad press, the food of last resort. 'What have you got in the cupboard?' 'Only a can of tuna I'm afraid.' The diners groan, throw a lettuce leaf and a tomato at it and dream of proper food. This is to do tuna a disservice. In the following pages we aim to show tuna's true versatility with almost a hundred recipes ranging from soups to pasta dishes, salads to casseroles, pates to fondue.

Read, cook and inwardly digest!

SOUPS AND STARTERS

TUNA AND CELERY SOUP

14 oz (400 gms) tuna in brine
12 oz (350 gms) celery, roughly chopped
4 tomatoes, peeled and diced
2 oz (50 gms) onion, chopped
1 clove garlic, crushed
¾ pint (450 ml) boiling water
1 pint (570 ml) skimmed milk
1 blade mace
1 bay leaf
4 tsp cornflour
parsley
salt and pepper

Place the tuna, celery, tomatoes, garlic, mace and bay leaf in a large saucepan. Bring to the boil and simmer for twenty minutes. Remove the mace and bay leaf and then blend the broth in a liquidiser and until smooth.

Mix the cornflour with a little of the soup to make a smooth cream. Pour the broth to a clean saucepan, add the cornflour cream and stir over a low heat until it thickens. Season to taste and garnish with chopped parsley or fresh coriander.

TUNA AND SWEETCORN SOUP

7 oz (200 gms) tuna in brine
1 tsp hot curry powder
3 tbls flour
1 oz (25 gms) butter
2 cups of chicken stock
1 cup milk
4 oz (100 gms) can of sweetcorn
2 tbls sherry
parsley

Melt the butter in a frying pan and cook the flour and curry powder gently over a low heat. After a couple of minutes add the chicken stock and then the milk to create a thin, smooth sauce. Bring to the boil and simmer for several minutes. Remove from the heat and add the flaked tuna and rained sweetcorn. Heat through again and, just before serving, add a dash of sherry or brandy and garnish with parsley.

TUNA CHOWDER

7 oz (200 gms) tuna in brine
2 rashers of bacon, chopped
1 small onion, finely chopped
1 oz (25 gms) butter
1 pint (570 ml) fish stock or water
2 tsp lemon juice
1 large potato
1 oz (25 gms) flour
½ pint (275 ml) milk
6 tbls single cream
salt and pepper
parsley
2 tbls sweetcorn

Heat the butter in a heavy based saucepan. Add the bacon and onion and cook until the onion is soft. Add the fish stock and lemon juice and bring to the boil. Add the potato and tuna and simmer for about ten minutes or until the potato is cooked. Blend the flour with the milk. Remove the soup from the heat and stir in the flour and milk mix, then return to the heat, stirring continuously until thickened. Remove from the heat and stir in the cream. Garnish with parsley and sweetcorn and serve immediately.

TUNA AND SALMON SOUP

7 oz (200 gms) tuna in brine
7 oz (200 gms) tinned salmon
2 lbs (900 gms) tomatoes
1 red pepper
1 cucumber
1 clove of garlic
2 tbls white wine vinegar
¼ cup olive oil
4 drops tabasco sauce
1 onion
2 tbls fresh mint, chopped
juice of 1 lemon
salt and pepper

Skin and seed the tomatoes and then put them in a blender along with half the red pepper, half the cucumber and all the garlic. Puree into a fine paste, then add the vinegar, olive oil and tabasco sauce.

Dice the onion and the remaining red pepper and cucumber. Place in a bowl and refrigerate.

Flake the tuna and salmon and season with salt and lemon juice. Place the fish mixture into chilled soup bowls, pour over the vegetable puree, and sprinkle with diced chilled diced vegetables. Garnish with mint and serve.

TUNA CAPERS

7 oz (200 gms) tuna
6 hard boiled eggs, chopped
tomatoes, finely chopped
2 tbls capers
¼ pint (150 ml) single cream
½ pint (300 ml) mayonnaise
juice of a lemon
1 tbls powdered gelatin
3 tbls water

In a mixing bowl, combine the mayonnaise, cream and lemon juice. Dissolve the gelatin in hot water, allow it to cool and then add it to the cream mixture. Stir in the flaked tuna, eggs, tomatoes and capers. Pour the mixture into individual ramekins and chill before serving.

*VGM TUC

TUNA CANAPES

7 oz (200 gms) tuna
2 tbls olive oil
1 tbls wine vinegar
1 tsp mustard
½ cup tomato ketchup
2 tbls onion, minced
salt and pepper
1 loaf of French bread

In a blender, make a dressing from the olive oil,
vinegar, mustard and tomato ketchup. Add to this
the flaked tuna and onion. Season to taste and serve
on toasted slices of French bread.

Double eaten by
11 on Tue bix

AVOCADO WITH TUNA

4 ripe avocados
7 oz (200 gms) tuna
8 oz (225 gms) mushrooms
4 oz (100 gms) butter
2 oz (50 gms) flour
1 pint (570 ml) milk
4 oz (100 gms) mature cheddar cheese, grated

Melt half the butter in a frying pan and saute the mushrooms until tender. Cut the avocados in half and scoop out the flesh. Keep the skins to one side.

Melt the remaining butter in a saucepan and stir in the flour. Cook gently for a couple of minutes before stirring in the milk to make a white sauce. Add the cheese, then fold in the chopped avocado flesh, flaked tuna and the mushrooms. Allow to cool and then spoon into the avocado skins. Place these on a baking tray and cook in a moderate oven - gas mark 4 (350f - 180c) for about 25 minutes.

TUNA MOUSSE

7 oz (200 gms) tuna
1 lb (450 gms) cottage cheese
4 oz (100 gms) cheddar cheese, grated
½ oz (10 gms) gelatin
1 chicken stock cube
3 tbls plain yoghurt
2 tsp parsley

Dissolve the chicken stock cube in a little boiling water and add the gelatin. Mix together the flaked tuna, cheese and yoghurt, fold in the gelatin mixture and the parsley. Refrigerate for at least one hour before serving.

21

TUNA COCKTAIL

7 oz (200 gms) tuna chunks in oil
1 can of peach slices
1 tbls cider vinegar
2 tbls plain yoghurt
6 small gherkins
4 oz (100 gms) bean sprouts
salt and pepper

Drain the tuna and peaches and reserve their oil and juice respectively. Whisk together one tablespoon of the tuna oil, two tablespoons of the peach juice and one tablespoon of cider vinegar. Mix in the yoghurt and seasoning. Toss the tuna, peach segments and gherkins in this dressing.

Line individual serving dishes with bean sprouts and pile the tuna-peach mixture on top. Chill and serve.

CHEESE AND TUNA MOUSSE

7 oz (200 gms) tuna
4 oz mature cheddar cheese, grated
2 tbls Parmesan cheese
2 eggs, separated
2 tsp mustard
½ pt (275 ml) double cream
Cayenne pepper

Whisk the egg yolks until pale and fluffy. Mix in the two cheeses, mustard and a generous pinch of cayenne pepper. Whip the cream until it peaks and fold it into the cheese mix, then add the flaked tuna. Whisk the egg whites until stiff and then fold them in to the above. Transfer to individual ramekins and chill thoroughly before serving.

TUNA AND SPINACH TERRINE

7 oz (200 gms) tuna
1 lb (450 gms) chopped spinach, frozen or tinned
2 oz (50 gms) butter, melted
8 oz (225 gms) cream cheese
¼ pint (150 ml) double cream
juice of 1 lemon
nutmeg
1 tbls powdered gelatin
4 tbls water
salt and pepper

Cook spinach (if frozen) and drain well on kitchen towels. Mix the spinach with the melted butter and season with nutmeg, salt and pepper. Dissolve the gelatin in hot water and add half of this to the spinach mixture.

Put the tuna, cream cheese, cream and lemon juice into a blender and puree. Transfer to a bowl and stir in the remaining gelatin.

Grease a small bread tin and cover the bottom with half the spinach mixture. Follow this with half the tuna mix, then another layer of spinach, ending with a layer of tuna. Refrigerate for several hours, then turn out onto a plate, slice and serve.

TUNA PATE

7 oz (200 gms) tuna
4 oz (100 gms) black olives
1 egg yolk
2 cloves garlic
2 oz (50 gms) capers
3 anchovy fillets
olive oil
salt
tabasco sauce

Combine the tuna, olives, garlic, capers and egg yolk
in a blender. Add a little olive oil as you work the
mixture, to produce a rich and smooth paste. Season with salt, pepper and tabasco sauce. Serve chilled
with warm toast.

PANSANELLA

6 slices white bread
1 large onion, finely chopped
6 oz (150 gms) ripe tomatoes
7 oz (200 gms) tuna in oil
1 small green pepper, diced
1 small red pepper, diced
2 spring onions, finely chopped
1 cucumber, diced
salt and pepper
vinaigrette dressing

Cut the crusts off the bread, tear into chunks, andsprinkle with enough water to moisten. Squeeze out any excess water and mix in the finely chopped vegetables Flake the tuna and add to mixture, then add vinaigrette and seasoning to taste. Chill well, sprinkle with parsley and serve.

TUNA AND COD SAVOURY

7 oz (200 gms) tuna in oil
7 oz (200 gms) cooked cod
½ oz (12.5 gms) gelatin
2 tbls water
1 cup mayonnaise
salt and pepper
7 oz (200 gms) chilled evaporated milk
1 tbls lemon juice
2 tsp oil
2 tsp lemon juice
1 lb tomatoes, peeled and quartered
6 spring onions
1 cucumber, thinly sliced

Dissolve the gelatin in hot water. Combine the tuna and its oil with the cod, mayonnaise, season well then stir in the dissolved gelatin. Whisk the evaporated milk with lemon juice until thick, then fold it into the fish mixture. Pour into a 2 pint ring mould and chill in the refrigerator until set.

Combine the oil and lemon juice in a mixing bowl and toss tomatoes and spring onions in this dressing

Remove the now set tuna-gelatin ring from the fridge and turn onto a serving dish. Fill the centre with the tomato and onion mixture. Garnish with cucumber rings and serve.

TUNA AND PISTACHIO PATE

7 oz (200 gms) tuna in oil
3 tbls brandy
2 hard boiled eggs, chopped
6 oz (175 gms) cream cheese
4 tbls pistachio nuts, coarsely chopped
horseradish sauce
black pepper

Break up the tuna with a fork and blend it with the tuna oil and brandy. Add the egg, cream cheese and pepper. Blend into a smooth paste and then add the pistachio nuts. Spoon into a suitable sized ramekin and refrigerate until firm. Serve with crackers or warm French bread.

SNACKS AND LIGHT MEALS

TUNA AND 3 BEAN PITTA POCKETS

8oz (225 gms) can of chick peas
8 oz (225 gms) can of red kidney beans
8 oz (225 gms) can of haricot beans
14 oz (400 gms) tuna in oil
small green pepper, sliced
3 tbls mayonnaise
3 oz (75 gms) chopped cashew nuts
Juice of 1 lemon
4 pita bread, sliced into pockets

Drain the beans and turn into a mixing bowl. Add the peppers, flaked tuna, cashew nuts, mayonnaise, and the lemon juice. Stir the ingredients well and serve in the warmed pita pockets.

TUNA AND SESAME KOFTAS

4 medium potatoes
14 oz (400 gms) tuna in oil
1 egg yolk
4 spring onions, finely chopped
1 stick celery plainflour
1 egg, lightly beaten
1 tbls milk
¼ cup bread crumbs
¼ cup sesame seeds
½ pints (1 litre) vegetable oil

Boil the potatoes until they are tender, drain, mash and allow to cool for a few minutes. Stir in tuna, egg yolk, shallots and celery. Cover and refrigerate for 15 minutes.

Flour hands and roll small quantities of the tuna mixture into balls. Dip these koftas into egg and milk, then roll in a mixture of bread crumbs and sesame seeds. Deep-fry, a few at a time, in very hot vegetable oil until golden brown, drain on kitchen towels. Serve hot or cold as a savoury snack.

PAN BAGNA

14 oz (400 gms) tuna in oil
1 French baguette
salt and coarse black pepper
1 tbls red wine vinegar
3 tbls olive oil
1 head lettuce coarsely shredded
2 ripe tomatoes, sliced
1 large onion, chopped
4 oz (100 gms) anchovy fillets
1 cup olives

Split the baguette horizontally and place each half on a separate sheet of kitchen foil. Cover the bread with a layer of flaked tuna. In a mixing bowl, combine salt and pepper, vinegar and olive oil, then turn the lettuce, tomatoes and onion in this dressing. Pile this mixture over the tuna and top with the anchovy fillets and olives. Wrap each half of the baguette tightly with the aluminium foil, turn upside down and allow to stand for several hours, so that the tuna mixture permeates the bread.

Cut into halves and serve with a crisp salad.

4 sli
1 pkt whi
½ pt (2 75
7 oz (200 gms) tu
2 oz (50 gms) cheddar che
paprika pepper

Toast bread on both sides and keep w
up the white sauce and add coarsely fla
together with its oil. Reheat gently, taking ca
to break up the fish. Spoon mixture onto the to
sprinkle with grated cheese and paprika and plac
under a hot grill for a couple of minutes, until the
cheese has melted and is golden.

NA AND ANCHOVY EGGS

6 hard boiled eggs
2 oz (50 gms) butter
2 oz (50 gms) tuna
4 anchovy fillets, chopped
black olives, minced
paprika

Cut the hard boiled eggs in half and scoop the yolks into a mixing bowl. Mash the yolks together with the tuna, anchovies and olives until they form a smooth paste. Spoon or pipe the mixture back into the egg whites; sprinkle with paprika and serve.

TUNA BURGERS

7 oz (200 gms) tuna in oil
4 large potatoes, cooked and mashed
2 onions, finely chopped
4 oz (100 gms) celery, finely chopped
1 tbls capers
2 anchovy fillets
1 tbls parsley, chopped
1 tsp worcestershire sauce
1 tsp lemon rind, grated
seasoned flour
salt and pepper
vegetable oil

In a large mixing bowl, mash the tuna in its own oil. Add the potatoes and the other ingredients, with the exception of the flour and oil, and season to taste. Form the mixture into six patties, dust with flour, brush lightly with oil and place under a moderate grill. Allow about five minutes per side for the burgers to heat through and brown.

SPINACH, TUNA AND FETA SAMOSAS

8 oz (225 gms) spinach, frozen or tinned
4 oz (100 gms) feta cheese
4 oz (100 gms) cream cheese
14 oz (400 gms) tuna
3 tbls lemon juice
1 tbls mayonnaise
10 sheets filo pastry
¼ cup olive oil

Chop spinach and drain thoroughly on paper towels. In a mixing bowl, blend together the cheeses, tuna, lemon juice and mayonnaise until smooth, then stir in spinach.

Brush each sheet of filo pastry with a little oil, and layer 2 sheets together. Fold the 2 layered sheets in half, cut into 4 pieces and then repeat the process with remaining pastry.

Place about 2 level teaspoons of the tuna mixture across one corner of each piece of pastry, then roll up each piece, tucking in the ends. Brush each parcel lightly with oil, place on a baking tray and bake in a hot oven for about 20 minutes.

TUNA VOL-AU-VENTS

2 doz frozen vol-au-vent cases
4 oz (100 gms) tuna
2 anchovy fillets, chopped
2 tbls soft butter
black pepper
1 tsp lemon juice
1 tsp grated onion
parsley

Bake the *vol-au-vent* cases according to the manufacturer's instructions. Blend the tuna, anchovy, butter, pepper, lemon juice and onion until they form a smooth paste. Scoop a heaped teaspoon of the mixture into each *vol-au-vent* case and garnish with a small sprig of parsley.

TUNA ON FRIED BREAD

1 French bread stick
7 oz (200 gms) tuna
4 tsp white wine vinegar
2 tbls onion, finely chopped
4 tsp mayonnaise
1 hard boiled egg yolk
2 dill pickles
vegetable oil
salt and pepper

Cut the French loaf into quarter inch slices. Heat the oil in a skillet and fry the bread slices until golden. Drain the slices thoroughly on paper towels. In a mixing bowl, combine the tuna, vinegar, onion, salt and mayonnaise. Pile on to fried bread and serve with egg yolk on top. Garnish with pickle slice and dab of mayonnaise.

TUNA NESTS

2½ lbs (1 kg) potato, cooked and mashed
14 oz (400 gms) tuna in brine
4 oz (100 gms) mature cheddar, grated
7 oz (200 gms) can baked beans
6 spring onions, finely chopped
salt and pepper

Beat the mashed potato and cheese together, then spoon the mixture into a piping bag with a large star nozzle. Pipe four oval potato nests on to four plates. Place these under a moderate grill for about five minutes, or until they are warmed through and browned.

In a saucepan, heat the beans, flaked tuna and spring onions. Spoon the mixture into the potato nests and serve immediately.

TUNA FRITTATA

7 oz (200 gms) tuna
7 oz (200 gms) sweet potatoes
2 oz (50 gms) butter
1 medium onion, chopped
1 large tomato, chopped
2 tbls parsley
2 eggs, beaten
2 tbls orange rind, coarsely grated
4 oz (100 gms) cheddar cheese, grated

Boil the sweet potatoes until tender; drain and place in water for about ten minutes to cool; drain again. Melt half the butter in small frying pan, add onion and sweat until soft; add tomato and simmer for about five minutes until the mixture has thickened slightly. Place tomato mixture in a bowl to cool. Peel the sweet potatoes and cut them into chunks; add to tomato mixture along with the flaked tuna, parsley, eggs, orange rind and grated cheese.

Heat remaining butter in a frying pan, add the tuna-sweet potato mixture, cook over medium heat for about three minutes, until base is cooked and lightly browned, then place the pan under hot grill for a further three minutes or until the surface is golden brown and the eggs are fully cooked.

Allow to cool for a couple of minutes and then cut into wedges and serve with a green salad.

TUNA VOL-AU-VENTS 2

7 oz (200 gms) tuna in oil
24 vol-au-vent cases
4 tsp dill pickle, minced
2 tbls tomato sauce
½ tsp white wine vinegar
1 tbls capers, chopped
1 tsp minced onion
3 tbls minced hard-boiled egg
½ tsp chopped capers
cayenne pepper
salt and pepper
green olives with pimento, chopped

Combine all the ingredients except the *vol-au-vent* cases and the olives. Allow the mixture to stand for at least two hour for the flavours to mature.

Cook the *vol-au-vent* cases according to the manufacturer's instructions. Allow them to cool and then fill with the tuna mixture and garnish with chopped olives.

MEXICAN TUNA GRILL

7 oz (200 gms) tuna in oil
½ cup green chillies, chopped
4 tbls onion, finely chopped
½ cup sour cream
½ cup cheddar cheese
¼ cupfresh coriander
12 slices wholemeal bread
butter
salt and pepper

Mix together the tuna, chillies, onion, sour cream, cheese and coriander. Spread the mixture onto six of the slices of bread. Complete the sandwiches with the remaining six slices.

Coat the outside of the sandwiches with butter and fry on both sides for about four minutes, or until the bread is golden brown.

EGG, TUNA AND HAM SAVOURIES

4 hard-boiled eggs
6 tsp mayonnaise
4 oz (100 gms) mashed tuna
4 large, thin slice boiled ham cut in 8 long strips
chopped parsley

Cut the eggs into halves and top each with a level teaspoon of the mayonnaise, followed by a heaped teaspoon of the tuna. Wrap a strip of ham around each individual egg half and secure with a toothpick. Sprinkle with parsley and serve chilled.

TUNA TACOS

7 oz (200 gms) tuna
8 oz (225 gms) tin taco sauce
½ tsp garlic salt
½ cup shredded iceberg lettuce
6 tacos shells, heated
1 cup cheddar cheese, grated
1 large tomato, chopped
1 ripe avocado, peeled and chopped
½ cup green onions, chopped

Mix together the tuna, taco sauce and garlic salt. Place a layer of chopped lettuce in each taco shell. Spoon about half a cup of the tuna mixture into each shell, and top with tomato, cheese, avocado and green onions.

SALADS

TUNA ASPARAGUS SALAD

1 bunch fresh asparagus
14 oz (400 gms) tuna
4 oz (100 gms) tin mushrooms
1 red pepper, finely sliced
1 small cucumber, sliced
1 lettuce
3 hard boiled eggs, sliced
2 tbls white vinegar
½ cup olive oil
1 red onion, finely chopped
1 clove garlic, chopped
3 spring onions, finely chopped

Boil asparagus until tender, rinse under cold water and drain. Combine asparagus, tuna, mushrooms, pepper, cucumber, lettuce and eggs in a salad bowl.

Combine vinegar, oil, onion, garlic and shallots in a jar, shake well and drizzle over the salad just before serving.

TUNA AND BACON SALAD

14 oz (400 gms) tuna
1 cup sour cream
1 large head of lettuce, shredded
2 carrots, cut into fine strips
1 cucumber, sliced
4 spring onions
½ cup mayonnaise
½ cup milk
¾ cup crumbled bacon
6 radishes, finely sliced
3 tbls Italian dressing

Combine the cream, mayonnaise and Italian dressing, then gradually add milk, stirring until smooth. Line a large salad bowl with lettuce and arrange tuna, carrots, cucumber, onions and radishes on lettuce bed. Sprinkle with bacon bits and drizzle with dressing.

JA AND BEAN SALAD

7 oz (200 gms) tuna
8 oz (200 gms) can of haricot beans
3 tbls olive oil
1 tbls wine vinegar
salt and ground pepper
1 medium onion, finely sliced
¼ cup fresh parsley, chopped

Simmer the beans in boiling water for a couple of minutes and then turn into a mixing bowl. Combine the oil, vinegar, salt and pepper and mix with the still warm beans. Allow to cool for 15 minutes, then carefully mix in the onion and tuna. Taste and adjust seasoning. Transfer to a shallow serving dish, sprinkle liberally with parsley and serve.

SALADE NICOISE

1 small cucumber
4 tomatoes, thickly sliced
6 oz (150 gms) broad beans
4 small artichokes, quartered
1 fennel bulb, thinly sliced
2 green peppers, sliced
1 doz radishes, quartered
2 hard boiled eggs, quartered
12 anchovy fillets
14 oz (400 gms) tuna in oil
4 oz (100 gms) black olives
assorted lettuce leaves
8 tbls olive oil
salt and pepper
2 cloves of garlic, crushed
12 leaves fresh basil

Peel and slice the cucumber and drain on a paper towel. Arrange the vegetables, eggs, anchovy fillets, tuna and olives attractively in a wide, shallow dish, then surround with lettuce leaves.

Mix the oil, salt, pepper, garlic and basil. Pour over the salad without stirring. Toss lightly just prior to serving.

ROMAN TUNA SALAD

7 oz (200 gms) tuna
1 head of lettuce
6 new potatoes, boiled and sliced
4 ripe tomatoes, sliced
12 olives, quartered
2 stalks of celery, sliced
7 oz (200 gms) tuna in oil
salt and ground pepper
2 tbls lemon juice
6 tbls olive oil
6 anchovy fillets, chopped
2 tbls parsley, chopped

Line a large salad bowl with the lettuce leaves. Over this bed place a layer of sliced potatoes, a layer of sliced tomatoes; sprinkle with olives, celery and tuna just before serving.

Combine the lemon juice, olive oil, chopped anchovy fillets and parsley, and season to taste with salt and pepper. Pour this dressing over the salad and toss.

TUNA AND DILL SALA

7 oz (200 gms) tuna
2 oz (50 gms) diced celery
1 oz (25 gms) fresh dill, chopped
2 tbls fresh parsley, chopped
2 tbls chives, chopped
2 tbls mayonnaise
2 tbls yoghurt
1 tsp dijon mustard

Place the tuna in a mixing bowl and mash coarsely with the back of a fork. Stir in the celery, dill, parsley and chives, then spoon in the mayonnaise, yoghurt and mustard. Mix thoroughly but gently and serve chilled on a bed of crisp lettuce.

TUNA WITH BASIL AND ANCHOVY

14 oz (400 gms) tuna in oil
14 oz (400 gms) penne (quill-shaped pasta)
2 tbls olive oil
14 oz (400 gms) tuna
1 red pepper, chopped
1 green pepper, chopped
4 ripe tomatoes, quartered
4 oz (100 gms) black olives
1 tbls toasted pine kernels
salt and pepper
1 cup mayonnaise
4 tbls chopped fresh basil
12 anchovy fillets, chopped

Cook the pasta according to manufacturer's instructions, drain and rinse with cold water, toss in olive oil. Add the tuna, peppers, tomatoes, olives and pine kernels to the pasta. Season and mix carefully.

Mix together the mayonnaise, chopped basil and anchovy fillets. Chill for at least half an hour before mixing into the salad and serving.

TUSCAN TUNA SALAD

7 oz (200 gms) tuna in oil
14 oz (400 gms) can cannellini beans
6 spring onions, chopped
salt and ground pepper
4 tbls olive oil
1 tbls red wine vinegar
1 cup parsley, chopped

Drain the tuna and beans and mix together in a bowl. Add the chopped onion, olive oil and vinegar. Combine well and allow to stand for at least an hour or two for the flavours to mature. Season to taste.

Immediately before serving on a bed of crisp lettuce, stir in half the chopped parsley and sprinkle the remainder over the top of the salad.

TUNA AND RICE SALAD

4 oz (100 gms) long grain rice
8 oz (225 gms) red kidney beans, drained
8 oz (225 gms) tinned sweetcorn
7 oz (200 gms) tuna
1 large red pepper, diced
2 tbls fresh parsley, chopped
salt and ground pepper

Cook rice in boiling salted water until tender but firm. Drain, rinse under cold water and then drain again. Place in a large mixing bowl and add the remaining ingredients. Mix thoroughly, season to taste and chill for at least an hour before serving.

TUNA AND BROWN RICE SALAD

7 oz (200 gms) tuna in oil
½ pint (275 ml) brown rice
1 pint (570 ml) boiling water
2 oz (50 gms) butter
4 anchovy fillets, chopped
2 tbls capers
juice of 1 lemon
2 tbls white wine vinegar
1 tsp Dijon mustard
salt and pepper

Melt the butter in a heavy bottomed saucepan and toss the rice until its is translucent. Pour in the boiling water, cover and simmer for about forty minutes, or until all the water has been absorbed.

Combine the oil, vinegar, lemon juice, and mustard and pour over the cooked rice while it is still warm. Allow to cool and then stir in the flaked tuna fish, capers, and chopped anchovies. Chill and serve with a green salad.

SWEET AND SOUR SALAD

7 oz (200 gms) tuna in oil
2 onions, finely chopped
2 tbls tomato puree
½ pint (275 ml) dry cider
¼ pint (150 ml) water
1 tbls brown sugar
2 tbls Worcestershire sauce
2 tbls mango chutney
2 tsps arrowroot
salt and pepper

Saute the onions in the oil from the tuna. When they are soft, add the tomato puree, cider, water, sugar, Worcestershire sauce, chutney, salt and pepper. Bring to the boil and simmer, uncovered, for about twenty minutes. Mix the arrowroot with a little of the juice from the pan and stir in until the sauce thickens. Season to taste and allow to cool.

Toss the tuna in the cold sauce and serve either on a bed of crisp lettuce or cold boiled rice.

PASTA AND RICE

PENNE WITH TUNA AND PEPPERS

7 oz (200 gms) tuna in oil
2 large red pepper
6 tbls olive oil
1 tbls garlic, chopped
3 tbls chopped parsley
2 tbls capers
salt
ground black pepper
1 lb (450 gms) penne (quill shaped pasta)
2 tbls fine lightly toasted bread crumbs

Preheat oven to its highest setting. Wash peppers, put on baking sheet, place on top shelf of the oven and bake until the skins are charred. remove and place in a plastic bag and allow to cool. When cool, remove the skins and then cut the flesh length ways into strips about half an inch wide.

Pour three tablespoons of olive oil into a saucepan, add garlic and cook until golden. Add the strips of pepper and cook for five minutes. Add the parsley and capers, stir a few times, then turn off the heat. Add the shredded tuna, season with pepper and salt and mix thoroughly.

Cook pasta according to manufacturers instructions, drain, then add the sauce. Toss, add the remaining olive oil, sprinkle with bread crumbs, and serve   immediately.

FETTUCCINE WITH TUNA AND GARLIC

7 oz (200 gms) can of tuna in oil
½ tsp chopped garlic
2 tbls parsley
1 egg beaten
2 oz (50 gms) soft butter
12 tbls double cream
salt
ground black pepper
3 oz (75 gms) freshly grated Parmesan
14 oz (400 gms) fettuccine

Drain tuna and turn into a mixing bowl. Add garlic, parsley, egg, butter, cream, salt, black pepper and cheese. Mix well then season to taste. Cook pasta according to manufacturer's instructions, drain, then toss immediately with tuna mixture. Sprinkle with cheese and serve at once.

TAGLIATELLE POINT LOMA

10 oz(300 gms) tagliatelle
½ oz (12 gms) butter
1 medium onion chopped
6 oz (150 gms) frozen peas
6 oz (150 gms) tinned sweetcorn
¼ pint chicken stock
1 tbls cornflour
300 ml fresh single cream
7 oz (200 gms) can of tuna
ground black pepper
3 oz (75 gms) grated Cheddar cheese

Cook pasta in boiling water for 8 to 10 minutes. Meanwhile melt butter and cook onion until soft, add the peas, sweetcorn and stock and cook for a further two minutes. Blend cornflour with a little water, then stir it into the vegetables along with the cream and tuna.

Cook gently until the sauce has thickened, then season to taste. Drain the pasta, stir into the sauce, and sprinkle with grated cheese.

TUNA AND PASTA WITH SOUR CREAM

8 oz (225 gms) pasta spirals or shells
7 oz (200 gms) tin of tuna, drained
4 hard-boiled eggs
1 oz (25 gms) butter
¼ pt sour cream
2 tsp anchovy essence
2 tbls vinegar
4 tbls chopped fresh chopped parsley
salt and black pepper

Cook pasta in a large pan of salted boiling water for about twelve minutes until *al dente*.

While the pasta is cooking, flake the tuna and chop the hard-boiled eggs. Melt the butter in a deep frying pan and toss the drained pasta: stir in the sour cream, anchovy essence and vinegar. Add the tuna and egg and parsley. Season well and warm over a low flame, stirring occasionally. Serve immediately with a crisp green salad.

TAGLIOLINI CON TONNO

7 oz (200 gms) tuna in oil
1 clove garlic, crushed
2 tbls chopped parsley, finely chopped
8 oz (225 gms) ripe tomatoes coarsely chopped
¼ pt (150 ml) chicken stock
salt and pepper
12 oz (350 gms) Tagliolini

Drain oil from tuna into a frying pan. Add garlic and saute for a couple of minutes. Add the parsley and tomatoes and simmer for ten minutes and when tomatoes begin to soften. Flake the tuna into the pan together with the stock, salt and pepper. Allow to continue simmering while the pasta is cooking.

Cook the pasta in boiling water with until it is *al dente*: drain well. Turn into a warm dish. Add the sauce, toss and serve immediately.

TUNA AND SWEETCORN LA

14 oz (400 gms) can chopped tomatoes with h
1 medium, chopped onion
2 oz (50 gms) mushrooms
1 medium green pepper, seeded and sliced
1 garlic clove crushed
14 oz (400 gms) of tinned tuna in brine
4 oz (100gms) canned sweetcorn, drained
4 oz (100 gms) ready to cook lasagne
2 tbls cornflour
½ tsp dry mustard
¾ pt fresh milk
2 oz (50 gms) grated mature cheddar cheese

Place the tomatoes, onion, mushrooms and garlic in a pan and bring to the boil. Simmer for five minutes and then stir in tuna and sweetcorn.

Blend together the cornflour, mustard and a little milk to make a smooth paste. Heat the remaining milk to boiling point, pour onto cornflour and stir well. Return to the heat and stir constantly until sauce thickens and is smooth, then stir in half the cheese.

Layer the tuna and vegetable mixture and lasagne in a 10 x 8 inch oven proof dish, then pour the cheese sauce over the top and sprinkle with remaining cheese. Bake at gas mark 6 (400f - 200c) for about 35-40 minutes.

TUNA LASAGNE 2

14 oz (400 gms) tuna in brine
14 oz (400 gms) tinned tomatoes
1 tbls tomato puree
1 tsp dried marjoram
6 oz (175 gms) oven ready lasagne
1 oz (25 gms) butter
4 tsp cornflour
½ pt (300 ml) milk
2 oz (50 gms) cheddar cheese
salt and pepper
2 tbls Parmesan cheese

Combine the tomatoes, tomato puree, marjoram, salt and pepper in a medium saucepan and simmer for thirty minutes. Add the tuna and continue to simmer for a few more minutes.

In a second saucepan, melt the butter and mix in the cornflour. Cook for one minute and then gradually add the milk, stirring continuously. When it has achieved a creamy consistency, add the cheddar cheese.

Arrange half the lasagne on the bottom of a greased oven proof dish. Pour in the tuna-tomato mixture and cover with the remaining lasagne. Pour the cheese sauce over the top and sprinkle with. Place in a moderate oven gas mark 6 (400F- 200C) and bake for about 35 minutes.

PASTA AND TUNA RAMEKINS

14 oz (400 gms) tuna
14 oz (400 gms) penne (pasta quills)
1 tbls olive oil
1 medium onion, diced
2 cloves of garlic, crushed
2 tbls tomato paste
14 oz (400 gms) can of tomatoes
4 oz can (100 gms) tomato puree
2 tbls chopped fresh chives
1 ½ cups grated Cheddar cheese
1 cup grated mozzarella cheese

Cook pasta in boiling water until tender, drain and leave to one side. Heat the oil in a large frying pan. Add the onion and garlic and stir constantly over a medium heat for a few minutes until onion is soft. Add the tomato paste, undrained crushed tomatoes and the tomato puree. Bring to boil, reduce heat and simmer for about fifteen minutes, until mixture is slightly thickened. Stir in the tuna, chives, cheddar cheese and finally the drained pasta.

Spoon mixture into six ramekins or small oven proof dishes. Sprinkle with mozzarella cheese, bake in moderate oven for about 15 minutes until lightly browned. Serve with a green salad.

CHEESE AND TUNA PENNE

7 oz (200 gms) tuna in oil
4 oz (100 gms) penne (pasta quills
2 tsp cornflour
12 ml oz milk
1 pinch of ground nutmeg
salt and ground black pepper
4 oz (100 gms) mature Cheddar cheese, grated
3oz (75 gms) sliced mushrooms
1 green pepper, chopped
1 red pepper, chopped
4 oz (100 gms) tinned sweetcorn

Cook pasta according to the packet instructions, drain well and set to one side.

Blend the corn flour with a little cold milk to make a smooth paste, then stir in the remaining milk. Heat, whisking continuously until sauce thickens; then add the nutmeg and season with salt and pepper. Add the cheese, vegetables, tuna and pasta. Mix thoroughly, heat through and serve immediately.

PASTA SUPPER

14 oz (400 gms) tagliatelle
1 oz (25 gms) butter
1 medium onion
8 oz (200 gms) frozen peas
4 oz (100 gms) tinned sweetcorn
¼ pt stock
1 tbls cornflour
10 ml oz fresh single cream
7 oz (200 gms) tinned tuna
ground black pepper
2 oz (100 gms) grated Cheddar cheese
Parmesan cheese

Cook pasta in boiling water for eight minutes, until it is *al dente*. Meanwhile melt butter in saucepan and saute the onion until soft. Add the peas, sweetcorn and stock; simmer for about two minutes. Blend the cornflour with a little water, and stir into vegetables together with cream, cheddar cheese and tuna. Cook gently until the sauce has thickened. Drain the cooked pasta and stir into sauce. Sprinkle with Parmesan cheese and serve.

TANGY TAGLIATELLE WITH TUNA

14 oz (400 gms) tagliatelle
7 oz (200 gms) tinned tuna
3 oz (75 gms) chopped walnuts
grated rind of 1 lemon
1 tsp worcestershire sauce
4 tbls chopped parsley
4 basil leaves
¼ pint (150 ml) olive oil
salt
freshly ground black pepper

Place the drained tuna, walnuts, lemon rind, worcestershire sauce and herbs into a food processor or blender and reduce to a smooth paste. Add the olive oil gradually, continuing to blend. Season to taste

Cook pasta according to package instructions. Drain and stir into the tuna sauce, taking care to coat each strand of pasta with sauce. Serve immediately with a crisp green salad and garlic bread.

SPAGHETTI WITH TUNA AND LEMON

14 oz (400 gms) spaghetti
2 tbls olive oil
1 clove garlic, crushed
4 tbls chopped parsley, finely chopped
7 oz(200gms) tinned tuna in oil
juice of 1 lemon
3 oz (75 gms) butter
salt and black pepper

Heat the olive oil and add the garlic and parsley. Stir continually over a low heat, gradually adding the drained and flaked tuna.

Cook pasta, following the manufacturer's directions. Drain and turn into a heated dish. Add the sauce and stir, then add the lemon juice, grated cheese, the butter divided into small pieces and salt and freshly ground pepper. Stir well and serve at once.

LINGUINE WITH TUNA AND TOMATO

14 oz (400 gms) linguine
2 tbls olive oil
1 medium onion, chopped
2 cloves of garlic, crushed
14 oz (400 gms) tin of tomatoes
salt and black pepper
7 oz (200 gms) tuna
2 tbls chopped capers
Parmesan cheese
4 tbls chopped parsley

Heat the oil and fry the chopped onion and garlic until softened. Add the tomatoes together with their juice; season with salt and pepper. Cook briskly for 10 minutes, stirring regularly. In a blender or food processor, render this to a paste and return it to the pan. Add the drained and flaked tuna and capers and cook for a further five minutes.

Cook the pasta following the manufacturers' instructions. Drain and add the sauce, stirring well. Add the chopped parsley and sprinkle with Parmesan.

TUNA AND NUT PILAF

14 oz (400 gms) tuna in oil
3 oz (60 gms) butter
1 medium onion, finely chopped
1 cup long grain rice
1 ½ cups water
2 small chicken stock cubes
1 bay leaf
½ cup sultanas
1 cup cooked green peas
½ cup roasted unsalted cashew nuts

Melt butter in medium saucepan, add the onion, and stir constantly over medium heat until onion is soft. Stir in the rice; add water, stock cubes, bay leaf and sultanas. Bring to the boil, reduce heat, cover tightly, and cook for approximately twenty minutes, until all liquid is absorbed and rice is tender. Using fork, gently fluff up the rice, then add the peas, cashews nuts and tuna. Mix carefully and serve at once.

TUNA RISOTTO

7 oz (200 gms) of tinned tuna in oil
1 chopped onion
2 rashers of streaky bacon ,diced
4 oz (100 gms) sliced mushrooms
8 oz (225 gms) long grain rice
2 tbls tomato puree
14 oz (400 gms) tin of tomatoes
½ pt (300 ml) vegetable stock
1 tbls lemon juice
tabasco sauce
2 oz (50 gms) frozen peas

Drain oil from tuna into a saucepan. Fry the onion, bacon and mushrooms in the tuna oil until tender. Add the rice, tomato puree, tomatoes, stock, lemon juice, tabasco and seasoning. Bring to boil, cover pan and simmer until rice is almost cooked. Add tuna and peas and continue cooking until rice is cooked and most of liquid has been absorbed. Serve with a tossed green salad.

TUNA RISOTTO 2

7 oz (200 gms) tuna in oil
3 oz (75 gms) butter
1 tbls olive oil
1 onion, chopped
1 clove garlic, crushed
9 oz (250 gms) long grain rice
1 ¾ pt (1 litre) chicken stock
4 oz (100 gms) assorted nuts
2 oz (50 gms) dates, chopped
3 tbls sweetcorn
parsley
salt and pepper

Heat the butter and oil in a heavy based saucepan.
Add the onion and garlic and saute gently until the
onion is soft but not browned. Add the rice and
continue to cook gently, stirring constantly, until
the rice is translucent. Add the chicken stock and
bring back to the boil. Cover the pan and simmer
gently until all the stock has been absorbed, about
25 minutes. Add the tuna, nuts, dates, and sweetcorn
and continue cooking for about three minutes.
Sprinkle with parsley and serve at once.

73

MAIN MEALS

TUNA CREOLE

4 oz (400 gms) tuna in brine
1 tbls oil
1 onion, finely chopped
1 green pepper, diced
1 green chilli pepper, finely chopped
1 stick celery, diced
1 tbls plain flour
14 oz (400 gms) can of tomatoes
2 tsp mixed herbs
Worcestershire sauce
8 oz (225 gms) long grain rice
½ pt (300 ml) water
salt and pepper

Heat the oil in a heavy bottomed frying pan. Add the onion, green pepper, chilli and celery, and saute over a low heat until soft but not browned. Stir in the flour and cook for two minutes. Add the tomatoes, herbs, lemon juice, seasoning and a couple of dashes of Worcestershire sauce. Bring to the boil and simmer for ten minutes. Add the tuna and cook for a further five minutes, without stirring.

Put the rice in a saucepan with a little salt. Pour in the water and bring to the boil. Cover tightly and simmer for about twenty minutes by which

76

time all the water should have been absorbed and the rice should be tender. Turn the rice onto a serving platter and top with the Creole sauce. Serve at once with a crisp green salad.

TRADITIONAL TUNA CASSEROLE

7 oz (200 gms) tuna in oil
4 oz penne (quill shaped pasta)
2 tbls onions, chopped
1 can cream of mushroom soup
1 cup crushed potato crisps, plain
2 tbls butter
2 sticks celery, chopped
½ cup milk
4 oz (100 gms) Double Gloucester cheese

Cook penne in boiling water until tender and drain thoroughly. Melt the butter in a heavy bottomed saucepan; add the onion and celery and cook until tender, but not browned. Add the soup, milk, cheese and heat until cheese is melted. Stir in the drained and flaked tuna. Place noodles in a casserole dish; add sauce and mix well. Sprinkle potato crisps over the top.

Bake for twenty minutes at gas mark 5 (190C - 375F).

BAKED TUNA AND AUBERGINE

7 oz (200 gms) tuna
2 large aubergines
salt
1 oz butter
1 large onion, finely chopped
1-2 chopped garlic cloves (depending on taste)
8 oz (200 gms) cooked brown rice
1 bay leaf, finely chopped
1 tsp lemon juice
6 tbls chicken stock
1 tsp tomato puree
8 oz (200 gms) Double Gloucester cheese, grated

Halve aubergines lengthwise and sprinkle the exposed flesh with salt. Allow to stand for thirty minutes; rinse and dry Scoop out the flesh leaving the skins intact. Chop the flesh into small chunks.

Melt the butter in a frying pan, add the aubergine flesh, onion and garlic and cook for five minutes stirring occasionally. Stir in the tuna, rice, bay leaf, lemon juice, stock, tomato puree and half the cheese.

Fill aubergine shells with the tuna mixture, top with the remainder of the cheese and place in an oven proof dish. Bake at gas mark 5 (375f- 190c) for twenty minutes, then cover with tin foil and bake for a further twenty minutes. Serve with a crisp green salad.

ORIENTAL TUNA CASSEROLE

14 oz (400 gms) tuna
14 oz (400 gms) can of cream of mushroom soup
¼ cup of water
1 tbls soy sauce
6 oz (150 gms) button mushrooms
2 cups tinned Chinese noodles
½ cup finely chopped green onions

Combine the flaked tuna, mushroom soup, water and soy sauce. Stir in the remaining ingredients and pour into a buttered oven proof dish. scatter the Chinese noodles over the top and bake at gas mark 6 (400f - 220c) for approximately forty minutes.

TUNA LOAF

14 oz (400 gms) tuna
1 can of cream of tomato soup
2 cups fresh bread crumbs
½ cup milk
½ cup minced pimento
3 tbls minced parsley
1 tbls salt
2 eggs beaten
freshly ground black pepper

Mash the tuna with the back of a fork and stir into the tomato soup. Soak the bread crumbs in milk and add tuna mixture, pimento, parsley, seasonings and eggs. Mix thoroughly, then place in a greased loaf pan and bake in a moderate oven - gas mark 5 (190c - 375f) for forty minutes. Serve hot or cold with fresh vegetables or a mixed salad.

TUNA LOAF 2

7 oz (200 gms) tuna
2 oz (50 gms) butter
1 onion, finely chopped
2 oz (50 gms) plain flour
13 ml oz (375 ml) milk
2 tbls mayonnaise
1 tsp Madras curry powder
juice of one lemon
chopped parsley
salt and pepper

Heat the butter in a heavy bottomed saucepan. Add the onion and celery and cook until soft but not browned. Add the flour and cook for a further minute stirring continuously. Gradually blend in the milk and stir until the sauce thickens. Remove from the heat and add the mayonnaise, curry powder, lemon juice, salt and pepper, parsley and tuna. Allow to cool and then beat in the eggs.

Pour the mixture into a greased loaf tin. Place in a moderate over - gas mark 5 (190c - 375f) - for about one hour. Leave to cool for a further hour before turning out. Slice and serve cold with a mixed salad.

TUNA AND MUSHROOM CASSEROLE

14 oz (400 gms) tuna in oil
4 tbls butter
4 tbls flour
fresh ground black pepper
2 cups milk
3 oz crushed potato crisps
1 cup of sliced cooked mushrooms

Melt butter in a heavy saucepan, blend in the flour and pepper; add milk gradually and cook until the sauce has thickened. Mix together half the potato crisps, tuna, mushrooms and sauce. Pour into greased casserole, cover with remaining crisps. Bake in moderate oven for thirty minutes.

CRUNCHY TOPPED TUNA BAKE

14 oz (400 gms) tuna in oil
1 medium onion, chopped
1 clove garlic, crushed
1 medium red pepper, chopped
2 sticks celery, chopped
1 tbls olive oil
14 oz (400 gms) can tomatoes
tabasco sauce
½ tsp sugar
3 tsp cornflour
½ cup water
2 tbls chopped fresh basil
paprika pepper
2 medium potatoes
1 cup mature cheddar cheese, grated
2 oz (50 gms) butter, melted

Cook the onion and garlic in olive oil until soft but not browned. Add red pepper and celery and cook for a further two minutes, stirring constantly. Stir in undrained crushed tomatoes, a generous splash of tabasco sauce and sugar. Bring to boil, and remove from heat.

Blend cornflour with water; add to tomato mixture. Bring to the boil and simmer gently, stirring continuously, until the sauce thickens. Stir in basil and flaked tuna. Spread mixture into a shallow dish.

Grate the potatoes coarsely and mix with the

cheese and butter. Spread this topping over the tuna mixture and place in a moderate oven - gas mark 5 (190c - 375f) for about thirty five minutes.

TUNA BALLS IN WHITE WINE

7 oz (200 gms) tuna
5 tbls bread crumbs
10 tbls chicken broth
10 tbls dry white wine
1 hard boiled egg, finely chopped
1 egg, lightly beaten
3 tbls minced parsley
2 large cloves of garlic, minced
salt and pepper
flour
2 tbls olive oil

Moisten bread crumbs with two tablespoons of the chicken broth and two tablespoons of white wine. Mix in the flaked tuna, hard boiled egg, beaten egg, parsley, salt and pepper.

Form the tuna mixture into one inch balls and dust with flour. Heat the oil in a frying pan and brown the tuna balls on all sides. Add the remaining chicken broth and wine, and season to taste. Cover the pan and simmer for about thirty minutes. Serve hot with rice or pasta, or cold as a savoury.

TUNA PROVENCALE

14 oz (400 gms) tuna in oil
4 oz (100 gms) pasta twists
two 14 oz (400 gms) tins ratatouille
1 tsp dried marjoram
4 oz (100 gms) mature cheddar cheese
salt and pepper

Cook the pasta twists in boiling salted water for about ten minutes; drain and set to one side. Combine the tuna, ratatouille and marjoram in an oven proof casserole dish. Season to taste and then add the cooked pasta. Mix gently and sprinkle with the grated cheddar cheese. Bake in a medium oven - gas mark 5 (190c - 375f) - for approximately thirty minutes or until the cheese is melted and golden. Serve with a green salad and crusty bread.

TUNA AND MUSHROOM PIZZA

12 inch oven-ready pizza base
7 oz (200 gms) passatta or chopped tomatoes
1 small onion, finely chopped
8 oz mozzarella or pizza cheese, sliced
1 tsp dried marjoram
1 tsp dried oregano
14 oz (400 gms) tuna in oil
1 small can anchovies (optional)
1 can of sliced mushrooms

Par-cook the pizza base in a medium oven for ten minutes. Allow to cool for about five minutes then coat with a layer of passatta or tomatoes. Sprinkle with chopped onions and then cover with a half the cheese slices. Over this arrange the tuna, mushrooms and anchovies. Sprinkle with marjoram and oregano and top off with a second layer of cheese.

Return to the oven for 10 minutes at gas mark 6 (200c - 400f). Serve with garlic bread and a green salad.

TUNA, LEEK AND MUSHROOM PIE

14 oz (400 gms) tuna in oil
2 leeks, sliced
2 oz (100 gms) butter
2 tbls plain flour
¼ pt (150 ml) milk
1 tbls olive oil
1 tsp dill
1 ½ lb (700 gms) of mashed potatoes
3 oz (75 gms) cheddar cheese, grated

V.g.

can mushrooms

Heat the olive oil in a heavy bottomed frying pan
and saute the leaks gently until tender. Set to one
side. Melt the butter, stir in the flour and cook for
1 minute. Drain the oil from the can and mix with
the milk. Gradually blend this into the roux. Bring
to the boil, stirring continuously, reduce the heat
and cook for a further minute, then stir in the dill.
Add the tuna to the sauce together with the leeks
and drained mushrooms. Season to taste. Pour this
mixture into a large shallow oven dish. Top with
mashed potatoes, and sprinkle with grated cheese.
Bake in a medium oven for thirty minutes until
golden brown.

VEAL WITH TUNA SAUCE

4 Veal escallops
7 oz (200 gms) tuna
1 oz (50 gms) butter
2 tbls oil
8 oz (225 gms) courgettes, sliced
1 large onion, sliced
8 oz (225 gms) baby carrots
1 pt (570 ml) chicken stock
10 fl oz (300 ml) soured cream
4 tsp cornflour
12 green olives, sliced
12 lemon slices

Beat the veal escallops until very thin and season with salt and pepper. Heat the butter and oil in a pan and saute the veal until browned on each side; remove from the pan and set to one side.

In the same pan, saute the courgettes, onion and carrots. After a few minutes, add the chicken stock, cover and simmer for ten minutes or until the carrots are tender.

Flake the tuna and combine with the cream. Add cornflour and blend until smooth, then add the tuna mixture to the pan and bring back to the boil. Replace veal and simmer for three minutes until hot. Garnish with olives and lemon and serve.

SCALLOPED TUNA AND POTATOES

6 potatoes, boiled
7 oz (200 gms) tuna in oil
1 tbls onion, chopped
1 can condensed celery soup
2 tbls olive oil
paprika pepper
salt

Slice potatoes and flake tuna, then fill a greased casserole dish with alternate layers of potatoes, tuna, onion and celery soup until all are used. Pour the olive oil over the top of the casserole and sprinkle with paprika. Bake in a hot oven - gas mark 7 (425f - 220c) - for about thirty minutes.

TUNA AND PAPRIKA BAKE

7 oz (200 gms) tuna
1 tbls butter
1 tbls flour
1 cup milk
salt and pepper
1 tsp paprika pepper
1 bay leaf
½ cup bread crumbs
2 hard boiled eggs
4 tbls lemon juice
1 tbls worcestershire sauce
4 oz (100 gms) grated cheese

Melt the butter in a saucepan. Blend in the flour, paprika and seasonings and gradually add the milk. Cook until thick and smooth, stirring constantly. Remove the bay leaf and add the flaked tuna, half the bread crumbs, eggs, lemon juice and worcestershire sauce. Pour into a two pint baking tin and top with remaining bread crumbs and cheese. Bake in a moderate oven for approximately 30 minutes. Serve with rice, pasta or a mixed salad.

TUNA SUPREME

7 oz (200 gms) tuna
1 cup mushrooms, sliced
2 tbls butter
1 tbls flour
1 cup milk
½ cup fresh bread crumbs
2 tbls chopped parsley
salt and pepper
2 eggs, beaten

Melt the butter in a saucepan and saute the mushrooms until soft. Blend in the flour and then gradually add the
milk. Simmer, stirring constantly, until the sauce thickens. Add the bread crumbs, tuna, parsley, seasoning and eggs. Pour this mixture into greased baking dish. Place this shallow pan of hot water and bake in moderate oven - gas mark 5 (375f - 190c) - for about forty minutes.

TUNA OMELETTES

7 oz (200 gms) tuna in brine
4 spring onions, finely chopped
4 tbls sour cream
8 fresh eggs
¼ pint (150 ml) milk
2 oz (50 gms) butter
salt and pepper

Mix the tuna and spring onions and season to taste, then stir in the sour cream.

To make one omelette, beat two of the eggs until frothy, then beat in a little seasoning and two tablespoons of milk. Melt a quarter of the butter in an omelette pan and roll the pan to ensure that the entire surface is coated. When smoking hot, pour in the eggs and cook over a high heat until they begin to set. Lift the edges of the omelette with a spatula to let any unset egg come in contact with the surface of the pan. When bubbling and brown underneath, spread one quarter of the tuna filling onto one side of the omelette. Fold the other side over, slide onto a warm plate and serve immediately. Make the remaining three omelettes in the same way.

TUNA AND OYSTER OMELETTE

7 oz (200 gms) tuna
8 eggs, separated
2 tbls water
2 oz (50 gms) butter
8 oz (200 gms) bean sprouts
6 oz (175 gms) smoked oysters
8 oz (200 gms) plain yoghurt
2 tsp mustard
2 tbls lemon juice
2 tbls chopped parsley
salt and pepper

Whisk egg whites with a pinch of salt until stiff, then whisk yolks with the water and pepper until frothy. Fold the yolks into the whites. Melt the butter in a heavy bottomed frying pan and add half the bean sprouts. Pour in half of the egg and allow to set. Add the remaining bean sprouts, then the remaining egg. Cook for about five minutes, lifting the edges occasionally with a spatula to allow the uncooked egg to come in contact with the pan.

Arrange the tuna around edge of omelette, with a ring of oysters inside. Put under a preheated grill for three or four minutes until golden.

Combine the yoghurt, mustard and lemon juice and pour this sauce over the omelette. Sprinkle with parsley, cut into wedges and serve immediately with a tomato and cucumber salad.

TUNA AND LEEK MUSHROOM BAKE

7 oz (200 gms) tuna in oil
1 small onion, chopped
1 clove garlic, crushed
2 large leeks, sliced
4 oz (100 gms) mushrooms
2 oz (50 gms) sweetcorn
8 oz (225 gms) pasta twists
½ pt (275 ml) milk
4 oz (100 gms) mature cheddar cheese, grated
1 oz (25 gms) plain flour
salt and pepper
cayenne pepper
4 oz (100 gms) gruyere cheese, grated
bread crumbs
olive oil

Cook pasta according to the manufacturer's instructions, drain and put to one side. In a frying pan, saute the garlic and onion until soft. Add the leeks and mushrooms and cook until tender. Stir in the flaked tuna and the sweetcorn and season to taste.

Heat the milk in a saucepan. Mix the flour with a small amount of water and pour this mixture into the warm milk and bring to the boil, stirring constantly until thick and creamy. Add cheddar cheese, season to taste with salt, pepper and cayenne pepper.

Mix the vegetable-tuna mix with the drained pasta and sauce; place in an oven proof dish. Mix together the gruyere cheese and bread crumbs and sprinkle over the top of the casserole. Bake in a pre-heated oven at gas mark 6 (400f - 200c) for about thirty minutes.

TUNA-STUFFED PEPPER

7 oz (200 gms) tuna in oil
2 large green peppers
2 oz (100 gms) brown rice
2 oz (100 gms) sweetcorn
4 tbls chicken stock
salt and pepper
2 lemon wedges

Boil brown rice in salted water for about thirty minutes, or until the grains are tender. Drain and allow to cool.

Slice the peppers in half lengthwise and remove the core and seeds. Blanch in boiling water for three to four minutes. Combine the rice, sweetcorn and tuna; add the stock and seasoning. Fill the pepper halves with the tuna mixture. Place in an oven proof dish and cover with kitchen foil. Bake in a moderate oven - gas mark 5 (375c - 190c) for thirty minutes. Garnish with a lemon wedge and serve with a mixed salad.

TUNA AND SPINACH BAKE

14 oz (400 gms) tuna
2 oz butter
1 medium onion, finely chopped
8 oz (225 gms) frozen spinach
1 cup mature cheddar cheese, grated
½ cup evaporated milk
3 eggs, beaten
½ cup bread crumbs

Melt the butter in a heavy bottomed frying pan and sweat the onions until they are soft. Add the spinach and heat through. Spread the spinach-onion mixture over the bottom of and oven proof casserole dish; cover this with flaked tuna, then pour over the combined eggs and milk. Sprinkle with the grated cheese and bread crumbs. Bake in a medium over for about forty minutes.

TUNA PAELLA

7 oz (200 gms) tuna in oil
4 oz (100 gms) tin smoked musse~
4 oz (100 gms) tin prawns
4 oz (100 gms) tin shrimps
1 large onion, finely chopped
9 oz (250 gms) tomatoes, peeled and chopped
4 oz (100 gms) frozen peas
1 teaspoon paprika pepper
2 cloves garlic, crushed
12 oz (250 gms) risotto rice
1 ¾ pts (1 litre) fish stock
¼ teaspoon powdered saffron
salt and pepper

Drain the tuna and the mussels and reserve their oils. Heat two tablespoons of this fish oil in a large heavy bottomed frying pan and saute the onion and garlic until soft but not browned. Add the tomatoes, paprika and seasoning. Simmer for about five minutes. Push the mixture to one side of the pan and fry the rice for two minutes, stirring constantly. Add the stock, bring to the boil and then stir in the saffron. Simmer, uncovered for, fifteen minutes. Gently stir in the tuna, shellfish and peas. Continue to simmer gently for a further five minutes. Serve immediately.

TUNA FONDUE

7 oz (200 gms) tuna chunks in brine
1 clove garlic
½ pint (275 ml) dry cider
1 tbls lemon juice
1 lb (450 gms) mature cheddar cheese, grated
1 tbls cornflour
1 oz (25 gms) butter
2 tbls Worcestershire sauce
2 tbls dry sherry
black pepper

Rub the inside of a fondue dish with garlic. Add the cider and lemon juice and heat gently. Combine the cheese, cornflour and butter. Add this mixture gradually to the warm cider. Season with pepper. Cook over a low heat stirring constantly, until the cheese has melted and the mixture has a achieved a creamy consistency. Stir in the Worcestershire sauce, sherry and tuna chunks. Serve with cubes of French bread, cucumber and celery.

CARIBBEAN TUNA CASSEROLE

14 oz (400 gms) tuna in oil
2 cups black-eyed peas
1 large onion, finely chopped
3 tbls olive oil
1 large, finely chopped
2 tsp dried chilli peppers, crushed
2 tbls tomato puree
½ cup bread crumbs
4 bananas
salt

Heat the olive oil in a casserole dish and on the stove top saute the onions until soft but not brown. Add the black-eyed peas, tomato and chilli peppers. Transfer to a medium oven and bake uncovered for fifteen minutes. Add the tuna, tomato paste and seasoning. Cover the dish and return to the oven for a further ten minutes. Remove cover and sprinkle with bread crumbs and bake for a further ten minutes until the bread crumbs are browned. Serve with baked bananas.

TUNA STUFFED COURGETTES

7 oz (200 gms) tuna in oil
1 ½ lbs (650 gms) large courgettes
1 lb (450 gms) ripe tomatoes
1 oz (25 gms) fresh bread crumbs
2 tbls chopped parsley
2 oz (50 gms) fresh Parmesan cheese, grated
6 tbls olive oil
black pepper

Soak the courgettes in cold water for about twenty minutes. Meanwhile peel and dice the tomatoes. Cut off and discard both ends of the courgettes; scoop out the flesh being careful to leave the outer wall in tact. Chop four ounces (100 gms) of the flesh finely and put to one side.

Soak the bread crumbs in water, squeeze dry and place in a mixing bowl. Add the grated cheese, tuna, chopped tomato, courgette flesh, parsley and black pepper. Mix thoroughly with a fork and return to the courgette skins.

Heat the olive oil in a heavy frying pan and saute the stuffed courgettes until brown. Remove with a slotted spoon and serve.

SAUCES AND DIPS

TUNA QUICHE

14 oz (400 gms) tuna
6 eggs
1 cup milk
1 tsp prepared horseradish
1 tbls lemon juice
½ tsp basil
salt
8 oz (225 gms) frozen peas, thawed
8 oz (225 gms) tinned water chestnuts
¼ cup spring onions, chopped
2 cups mature cheddar cheese, grated

Combine the eggs, milk, horseradish, lemon juice, salt and basil in a mixing bowl, then stir in the tuna, peas, chestnuts, onions and 1½ cups of cheese.

Pour the mixture into an shallow ovenproof dish. Sprinkle the remaining cheese over the top and place in a medium oven - gas mark 5 (375f - 190f) - for thirty minutes. Allow to stand for at least ten minutes before serving.

TUNA AND BROCCOLI BAKE

14 oz (400 gms) tuna in brine
1 lb frozen broccoli, cooked
4 oz (50 gms) butter
4 tomatoes, quartered
3 tbls flour
½ pint (275 ml) milk
1 tsp mustard powder
8 oz (200 gms) mature cheddar cheese, grated
salt and pepper

Arrange the cooked broccoli in the base of an shallow oven proof casserole dish and dot with half the butter. Place the tuna and tomato on top and season.

Melt the remaining butter in a saucepan. Add flour, mustard powder, salt and pepper. Cook for a couple of minutes and then gradually add the milk. Bring back to the boil, stirring constantly until the sauce thickens. Add most of the grated cheese and pour the sauce over the tuna-tomato mixture. Sprinkle the remaining cheese over the top and place in a moderate oven - gas mark 6 (400f - 200c) for about thirty minutes, or until golden brown.

TUNA PIE

7 oz (200 gms) tuna
½ cup onions, chopped
1 lb (450 gms) tinned tomatoes
4 oz (200 gms) tinned mushrooms
1 green pepper, chopped
4 eggs
½ cup milk
1 cup water
1 cup fresh bread crumbs
½ tsp garlic powder
¼ cup plain flour
2 tbls butter
1 tsp dried oregano
½ tsp dried basil
salt and pepper

Place the tuna, onions, mushrooms, tomatoes and green peppers in a greased oven pan.

Combine the eggs, milk, bread crumbs and other ingredients in a blender and work into a smooth paste. Pour the sauce over the tuna and vegetables, allow to stand for ten minutes, then transfer to a medium oven and bake for three quarters of an hour. Remove from the oven and allow to stand for a further ten minutes before serving.

TUNA AND CHEESE DIP

7 oz (200 gms) tuna in oil
4 oz (100 gms) cream cheese
1 cup sour cream
3 oz (75 gms) stuffed olives, finely chopped
2 tbls spring onions, chopped
2 tsp prepared horseradish
1 tsp worcestershire sauce
salt

Blend sour cream and cream cheese into a smooth paste; stir in the finely flaked tuna, olives, spring onions, horseradish and worcestershire sauce. Season to taste, cover and refrigerate for at least an hour before serving. This dip is ideal with savoury biscuits and *crudites*.

7 oz (200 gms) tuna in oil
½ can anchovy fillets
½ pint (275 ml) mayonnaise
1 tbls lemon juice

Combine all the ingredients in a blender and work into a smooth paste. If the consistency is too thick, add a little water and blend again.

This mayonnaise is an ideal for stuffed eggs and tomatoes or as an accompaniment for cold chicken.

TUNA, TOMATO AND GARLIC SAUCE

7 oz (200 gms) tuna
7 oz (200 gms) tinned tomatoes
1 clove garlic
½ tbls olive oil
½ tbls Italian seasoning
½ tbls tomato puree
parsley

Chop the garlic and fry in olive oil until golden brown. Add the tomatoes, tomato puree and Italian seasoning and simmer gently for about ten minutes. Add the flaked tuna and cook for a further five minutes. Serve with pasta of your choice or use as a savoury dressing with hard boiled eggs or cold vegetables.

TONNATO SAUCE

7 oz (200 gms) tuna in oil
4 egg yolks
¾ pint (500 ml) olive oil
½ can anchovies
black pepper

Place egg yolks in a basin. Add the olive oil gradually, whipping continuously until the mixture is thick and creamy. Mash the tuna and anchovy fillets and beat them into the sauce. Season to taste with freshly ground black pepper.

This sauce is traditionally served over cold sliced veal, garnished with capers and lemon, but it is also excellent with cold chicken or hard boiled eggs.

TUNA AND FRUIT SAUCE

7 oz (200 gms) tuna
2 dessert apples, diced
1 orange, in segments
1 banana, sliced
4 cups white cabbage, shredded
6 tbls sour cream
1 tbls milk
1 tbls lemon juice
1 tsp caster sugar
1 tbls mustard
salt and black pepper

Blend together the sour cream, milk, lemon juice, sugar and mustard. Season to taste. combine this with the tuna and fruit in a mixing bowl. Chill and serve on a bed of shredded white cabbage.

TUNA AND HERB SAUCE

7 oz (200 gms) tuna in oil
1 onion, finely chopped
1 clove of garlic, crushed
14 oz (400 gms) canned tomatoes
1 tbls tomato puree
4 tbls white wine
1 tbls freshly chopped basil
1 tbls freshly chopped parsley
salt and ground black pepper

Drain oil from tuna into a saucepan. Fry the onion
and garlic until tender. Stir in the tomatoes, tomato
puree, wine, herbs and seasoning. Bring to the boil,
and simmer for 10 minutes. Add the tuna and continue simmering for a further 5 minutes. Serve with
the pasta of your choice.

TUNA CHEESE SAVOURY

7 oz (200 gms) tuna
4 thick slices white bread
4 oz (100 gms) mature chedder cheese, grated
1/3 cup stuffed olives, finely chopped
1 tsp lemon juice
2 tbls mayonnaise
salt and black pepper

Drain tuna, mix in cheese, olives, lemon juice and
mayonnaise. Season to taste with salt and pepper.
Serve on toast.